Bigly

BIGLY

DONALD TRUMP IN VERSE

**Make Poetry
Great Again**

Selected and arranged by
ROB LONG
screenwriter and co-executive
producer of *Cheers*

REGNERY
PUBLISHING
A Division of Salem Media Group

Regnery® is a registered trademark of Salem Communications Holding Corporation

Cataloging-in-Publication data on file with the Library of Congress

ISBN 978-1-62157-730-0

Published in the United States by
Regnery Publishing
A Division of Salem Media Group
300 New Jersey Ave NW
Washington, DC 20001
www.Regnery.com

Manufactured in the United States of America

10 9 8 7 6 5 4 3 2 1

Books are available in quantity for promotional or premium use. For information on discounts and terms, please visit our website: www.Regnery.com.

Distributed to the trade by
Perseus Distribution
www.perseusdistribution.com

Bold train conductor

Shredding fake news to pieces

Trump is my daddy

—Milo Yiannopoulos

CONTENTS

LIFE

LOVE

BEAUTY

DEATH

A Prefatory Note

What Is Poetry Anyway?

H. W. Crocker III

I can hear the scoffers now: "Donald Trump, a poet? You must be joking. The man can barely spell his name. He doesn't read books—and brags about that fact. He's our least literary president since Andrew Jackson. He doesn't know the difference between a colon and semi-colon, let alone haiku and a sonnet. He's a tweeter, not a poet."

But, as so often, Trump's critics have, to use George W. Bush's word, misunderestimated him.

Never in American history has the White House been graced with a man so vivid in his use of metaphor (and in his hair style), a man so pithy he makes pith seem longwinded, a man who more than anything else is a poet for our time.

I challenge anyone to read this book and not come away shaking his head and muttering to himself, "Therein lies a poet, a great-heart, a glorious wordsmith for the ages. Now I see why all those pundits on the cable networks, men and women whose wit is no match for his own, engage in fake news. It's because they can't handle the truth; and the truth is: Trump is a great poet."

So I invite you to crack open this book and read, enjoy, and memorize this sprightly selection of Donald J. Trump's verse.

If you come into this as a doubter, I can only say, along with another famous poet, "Abandon all hope, ye who enter here."

FOREWORD

Toby Young

"**C**oncentrate on what you want to say to yourself and your friends," wrote Allen Ginsberg. "Follow your inner moonlight; don't hide the madness. You say what you want to say when you don't care who's listening."

I wonder if Donald Trump read those words as a young man at The Wharton School? Trump has confessed to not being much of a reader—"Mostly, I read contracts," he told the Brazilian magazine *Veja* in 2014—but no other poet of his generation exemplifies Ginsberg's philosophy more fully.

Trump doesn't just shoot from the hip, he is aggressively indifferent to the good opinion of the liberal intelligentsia. And don't start in with that line about how he obviously *does* care because if he didn't he wouldn't be so determined to let them know how little he cares. After all, don't all great artists struggle with the same paradox?

Trump wants to be noticed all right, but on his own maverick terms, not by sucking up to the literary establishment. All his life, he has marched to the beat of his own drum—something he has in common with Emerson, Whitman, and Frost—and what a drum it is, beating out those irregular, staccato rhythms. Trump is quite conventional in some respects, but his poetry belongs to the same free form, avant-garde tradition as Ginsberg. He is the heir to the beat poets, a glorious throwback to that era of unconstrained vitality in American letters. *Don't hide the madness.*

As a poet, Trump has not always been so direct and to the point. If you look at his early work—such as the forgotten gem "Table at Le Cirque," which he composed in 1984—it is more laid back and conversational than the abstract, pared-down poems of his late period, like "Truly Great," which he recited at a campaign rally in 2016. It is as if he has shifted from writing letters to barking out telegrams as his own mortality has begun to weigh on him.

Trump's impatience—his desire to fix the world's problems just as quickly as he possibly can—may be one of the reasons he is so at home in the spoken-word form, another debt he owes to Ginsberg. More than once Trump has compared himself to Ernest Hemingway and there is certainly something Hemingway-esque about his lack of regard for the usual namby-pamby trappings of literature. For him, there would be something unmanly about sitting down at a desk and carefully crafting a poem with quill and ink. No, the creative process has always been a hot, combustible one for him—more exclamation than composition. Trump may not wield a pen, but he is the lead in America's pencil.

Another symptom of his frontier spirit, his embodiment of a more rugged era in America's history, is his refusal to have any truck with irony. Trump *has* feelings, he does not quote them. There is no ironic distance in his free verse, no gradations of sincerity. He says what he means and means what he says. Such a refreshing alternative to the looping, self-referential solipsism of the post-modernist tripe that passes for poetry these days.

Another way in which Trump parts company from his fellow American poets is his extraordinary wealth. For a more delicate soul, the casinos and private jets, the fine food and beautiful women might have had a negative impact on the work, but not for Trump. On the contrary, his money has enabled him to get in touch with his animal side, to burrow down deep into his atavistic nature, and the result is a remarkably candid, down-to-earth body of work. Like an Oscar-winning Hollywood screenwriter, Trump has proven that you do not need to live in a garret to be a creative genius.

Not that Trump has won any prizes for his work. It is an ongoing scandal of American letters that the pointy-heads and high-ups who style themselves the guardians of good taste have refused to give Trump so

much as a Wallace Stevens Award, let alone a Pulitzer—
no, not even after he became president. To its eternal
shame, the Poetry Society of America has yet to
recognize the best contemporary practitioner of its art.
As George Orwell said, the greatest test of literary merit
is survival and we shall have to wait fifty, perhaps one
hundred years before Trump is given his due.

Yet in spite of all these slights, in spite of this ongoing
rejection by the intellectual elite, Trump has gloriously
risen above it all and just focused on the work. In his
most famous poem, Ginsberg said he had seen the best
minds of his generation destroyed by madness. Not so
in the case of Trump. His craziness is key to his survival.
No slings or arrows can penetrate that steel-like carapace
of self-confidence. As the great man himself would say,
"That I can tell you."

Our generation will be judged by the next generation
according to how we judged Donald Trump.

INTRODUCTION

The most important thing to keep in mind when developing real estate, as Donald Trump surely would agree, is that everything has to be built to code.

Fire sprinklers need to be in the right place, the wiring needs to be safely insulated, the structure needs to be sound—the requirements of real estate and construction allow for no improvisation, no loosely-goosey do-as-you-please.

Poetry, on the other hand, provides wide open spaces where the free expression of a complicated soul can burst out. Poetry, when practiced with joy and abandon, breaks rules. Great poetry, in other words, is rarely "up to code."

Perhaps this is why Donald Trump is so powerfully drawn to poetry. For it is here that the builder of the high-end golf club and the super-premium hotel and time-share resort can build Trump Towers of words and golf links of language—all without worrying about the building inspection. It is here, in the world of poetry and poetic expression, that Donald Trump can, metaphorically, unbutton the top button of his pants and just relax.

The Donald Trump that emerges from these spare, restrained poems is not the Donald Trump of the glamorous and gilded Trump Tower condominiums or the upper crusty Mar-a-Lago Golf Club. The man responsible for these compressed and pared-down poetic investigations into the nature of politics, romance, power, and finger size is not the man we see on the television, surrounded by gold leaf, celebrity lawyers, fine motor cars, and the trappings of the high life.

Donald Trump the Poet leaves the curlicues and frills to Donald Trump the Builder. Mar-a-Lago may be a place of fountains, marble-ite statues, and paintings of tigers, but the poems in this volume are marvels of economy and focus.

And honesty. There is, for instance, this achingly sad aside in his meditation on celebrity, "Can This Be a Normal Life":

Maybe it's the power that comes from having

The hottest show on television,

But people like me much better

Than they did before *The Apprentice.*

There is so much hurt there, buried in the bravado and the fanfare.

And here, in his intensely personal "My Hands Are Normal Hands," he allows himself to reveal this: "I buy a slightly smaller than large glove, okay?"

All of the poems in this collection are about, on one level, the quotidian events in the poet's life. But they are also about the poet himself. Or, rather, the subject of these poems is Donald J. Trump the public figure, as observed by Donald J. Trump the poet. The two are not one and the same. The poet sees the man beneath the gilding. The poet reveals the man beneath the orange.

"Society loves me," the poet writes in the razor-sharp near-haiku of "High Society." "And I can act differently / For different people."

Society may be fooled by the hype or dazzled by the glitz. But the poet knows his subject all too well, and is willing to reveal the many ways—both large and small—in which he is not quite up to code.

I.

LIFE

Mirth, with thee I mean to live.

—John Milton

My whole life is about winning.

—Donald Trump

The Lone Ranger

I understand

Life.

And I understand how

Life works.

I'm

The Lone Ranger.

April 2, 2016, interview with the Washington Post
*Discussing being singled out as the Republican nominee after being
in such a crowded field of candidates*

When I Was Young

You know,

When I was young and when I was—

Of course, I feel young.

I feel like I'm

30,

35,

39.

Somebody said,

Are you young?

I said,

I think I'm young.

You know, I was stopping—

When we were in the final month of that campaign,

Four stops,

Five stops,

Seven stops.

Speeches,

Speeches, in front of

25,000,

30,000 people,

15,000,

19,000

From stop to stop.

I feel young.

When I was young—

And I think we're all sort of young.

When I was young,

We were always winning things in this country.

We'd win with trade.

We'd win with wars.

At a certain age,

I remember hearing from one of my instructors,

"The United States has never lost a war."

And then,

After that,

It's like we haven't won anything.

We don't win anymore.

January 21, 2017, speech at CIA Headquarters
Langley, Virginia
First official visit to a government agency as president

Can This Be A Normal Life?

A businessperson on television

Has never had anything close to this

Success. It's like being a rock star. Six

People do nothing but sort my mail.

People come in and want my secretary

Robin's autograph. If a limo pulls up

In front of Trump Tower, hundreds of people

Gather around, even if it's not mine.

I ask, "Can this be a normal life?"

Maybe it's the power that comes from having

The hottest show on television,

But people like me much better

Than they did before *The Apprentice*.

And if you think about it, all I did

On the show was fire people, which proves

How bad my reputation must have been before this.

2004 Playboy *interview*

Editor's Note: *Here Trump effortlessly draws together three discrete images—six people sorting his mail, fans asking for his secretary's autograph, people crowding around any limo that comes close to Trump Tower—in a vivid and effective re-creation of his own experience with post-*Apprentice *fame.*

Elijah

He said,

You'll be the greatest president in the history of,

But you know what, I'll take that also,

But that you could be. But he said,

Will be the greatest president

But I would also accept the other.

In other words, if you do your job, but I accept that.

Then I watched him interviewed

And it was like he never even was here.

It's incredible. I watched him interviewed a week later

And it's like he was never in my office.

April 23, 2017, Associated Press interview
Washington, D.C.
Discussing a disputed conversation with Congressman Elijah Cummings

Live Like Kings

I really am tired of seeing

What's happening with this country—

How we're really making

Other people live like kings,

And we're not.

1988 interview on The Oprah Winfrey Show

The Bigness

Every agency is, like,

Bigger than any company.

So you know,

I really just see the bigness of it all,

But also the responsibility.

And the human responsibility.

You know, the human life that's involved

In some of the decisions.

April 23, 2017, Associated Press interview
Explaining that he never realized how big the presidency
was until taking office

A Straight Message

The media is going through

What they have to go through

To often times distort—not all the time—

And some of the media is fantastic,

I have to say—they're honest and fantastic.

But much of it is not a—the distortion—

And we'll talk about it,

You'll be able to ask me questions about it.

But we're not going to let it happen,

Because I'm here again,

To take my message straight to the people.

February 17, 2017, news conference
Announcing nominee for Secretary of Labor

The Border Wall

People want the border wall.

My base definitely wants the border wall,

My base really wants it—

You've been to many of the rallies.

Ok, the thing they want more than anything

Is the wall. My base, which is a big base;

I think my base is 45 percent.

You know, it's funny.

The Democrats, they have a big advantage

In the Electoral College. Big, big, big advantage.

I've always said the popular vote would be a lot easier

Than the Electoral College. The Electoral College—

But it's a whole different campaign—

The Electoral College is very difficult

For a Republican to win, and I will tell you,

The people want to see it.

They want to see the wall.

April 23, 2017, Associated Press interview
Washington, D.C.

Make America Great Again

We will make America proud again.

We will make America prosperous again.

We will make America safe again.

Friends and fellow citizens, we will make America

great again!

September 9, 2016, rally attended by 15,000 people
Fulfilling a promise to return to Pensacola, Florida following primary

Shaking Hands

It's not a healthy thing.

With the germs, it's not a question of "maybe"—

They have been proven, you catch colds.

You catch *problems*.

Frankly, the Japanese custom is a lot smarter.

May 13, 2011, interview with Rolling Stone *magazine*
Discussing his well-known aversion to shaking hands, which he has
since...shaken.

Editor's Note: *"You catch problems" is a classic Trump line—unusual*
yet perfectly to the point.

Call It Kobe

They're loaded, loaded with cars.

So they send millions of cars over here.

We sell them beef—beef.

They don't want it.

Half the time they send it back.

They want to send it back.

The farmers over there don't want it.

So we take it back.

That's not good beef

By the time you get it back.

I said the other day—

No, no, I say it's aged;

Now they call it Kobe beef

And we sell it for more money.

September 25, 2015, remarks at Values Voters Summit
Discussing trade with China

Editor's Note: *The power of this comedic poem is in its tempo: it begins in short, hard statements of fact then ends with a complex clause—like a series of perfect jabs leading up to a surprising right cross: "And we sell it for more money." This is Trump in fine form.*

Big League

What we do want to do is

We want to bring the country together,

Because the country is

Very,

Very

Divided,

And that's one thing I did see,

Big league.

It's very,

Very

Divided,

And I'm going to work

Very hard

To bring the country together.

Big League II

They're the forgotten people—

They were totally forgotten.

And we're going to bring jobs back.

We're going to bring jobs back,

Big league.

November 23, 2016, interview with the staff of the New York Times
New York Times *Headquarters*

Open Door

I want to keep that door open.

I have to keep that door open

Because if something happens

Where I'm not treated fairly

I may very well use that door.

August 11, 2015, interview with CNN's Newsday
Discussing the possibility of a third-party run

Editor's Note: *The image of "the door" is used to exquisite effect here, especially when Trump, the poet of possibility, notes "I may very well use that door."*

The Escalator Scene

And then the big thing,

By the way,

The big thing was standing

At the top of that escalator,

Looking down into that room—

Which was a sea of reporters,

Of which he was one, but a sea—

That was as big as anything we've had.

And getting up and saying, all right.

And I remember. I took a deep breath.

I said, "Let's go," to my wife.

And you know, we came down.

Pretty famous scene,

The escalator scene.

Boom.

*April 2, 2016, interview with Bob Woodward and Bob Costa
Discussing the day he announced his candidacy*

Editor's Note: *The imagery of descending to "a sea of reporters," and
the narrator reflecting to himself on how it was a "pretty famous
scene," effortlessly draws, from the literate reader, an image of
Captain Nemo and his submarine* The Nautilus, *down to the final,
classic Trump touch: "Boom."*

Modern Presidential

Okay, so my family

Comes up. Don.

My daughter Tiffany,

Who's a great kid.

Ivanka. My wife.

And we were together.

They said,

"Be presidential, Dad,

Be presidential."

Last debate.

I said,

Wait a minute.

If I get hit,

I'm going to hit back.

That's not going to look

Very presidential,

Because I hit back

And you hit back.

I said,

I'm going to give it a shot.

April 2, 2016, interview with the Washington Post
Discussing his combative tone in the presidential debates

The Dreamers

The dreamers we never talk about

Are the young Americans.

Why aren't young Americans dreamers also?

I want my dreamers

To be

Young.

Americans.

August 24, 2016, remarks
Jackson, Mississippi
Discussing children of illegal immigrants protected under the DREAM Act

Whining And Winning

I do whine,

Because I want to win,

And I'm not happy

About not winning,

And I am a whiner,

And I keep whining

And whining

Until I win.

August 11, 2015, interview on CNN

Editor's Note: *Typical of Trump's genius is to take two words so close in spelling (whining and winning), but so removed from each other in definition and to conflate them, in what literary critics call "alliterative onomatopoeia."*

Win So Much

We're going to win so much—

We're going to win a lot.

We're going to win a lot.

We're going to win so much

You're all going to get sick and tired of winning.

You're going to say oh no, not again.

I'm only kidding.

You never get tired of winning, right?

Never.

December 30, 2015
Speech in Hilton Head, South Carolina

Editor's Note: *Like a poetic magpie, Trump takes his inspiration from a wide variety of sources. Here, for instance, there's an unmistakable hint of hip-hop, if not rap.*

Reading

I don't read much.

Mostly I read contracts,

But usually my lawyers

Do most of the work.

There are too many pages.

February 2014 interview with Brazilian magazine Veja

Editor's Note: *Like Hemingway, Trump sees himself not merely, or even primarily, as a litterateur, but as a man of action.*

Table At Le Cirque

I know one man in particular.

He's one of the most successful men in New York,

And he couldn't get a table at a restaurant.

He's worth maybe four or five hundred million dollars,

And he's standing at Le Cirque or one of them

And he couldn't get a table.

So I see him standing there and he's a little embarrassed

And he says, "Don, could you help me get a table?"

So I got him a table. So he calls the next day and I said,

"No one knows you, you're very successful,"

And he says, "No, no no, I like to keep a low profile."

That's great. But in the meantime

He can't get a table in a restaurant.

November 11, 1984, interview with the Washington Post

My People

The people,

My people,

Are so smart,

And you know what they say

About my people?

(The polls.)

They say I have

The most loyal people—

Did you ever see that?

Where I could stand in the middle of 5th Avenue

And shoot somebody,

And I wouldn't lose any voters.

January 23, 2016, campaign rally
Sioux Center, Iowa

Editor's Note: *One of Trump's major themes, as illustrated in "Table at Le Cirque" and "My People," is the nature of post-modern life— both in the compromises that men must make, and the uses, even to an extreme, to which celebrity can be put. No poet has better captured this aspect of the twenty-first-century America than Trump.*

Jeb!

Well, I understand Jeb Bush.

I was rough with Jeb Bush.

And I think if I was Jeb Bush,

I wouldn't vote for me either.

May 8, 2016, interview on ABC's This Week
Responding to George Stephanopoulos's question about prominent Republicans refusing to endorse him

A Certain Position

While I've been president,

Which is just for

A very short period of time,

I've learned tremendous things

That you could only learn, frankly,

If you were in a certain position,

Namely, president.

February 10, 2017, news conference
Answering a question about his immigration executive order

New Hampshire

I was looking at very seriously

One time,

Not—they say, oh,

He looked at it for many—

I really, no.

I made a speech at the end of the '80s

In New Hampshire—

But it was really a speech that was,

It was not a political speech.

But because it happened to be

In New Hampshire—

April 2, 2016, interview with the Washington Post
Discussing when he became interested in entering politics

Editor's Note: *One does not always credit Trump with a haunting sense of place, but that is what he brilliantly evokes here with that closing line "In New Hampshire"—a state that changes everything that is said and done within its borders.*

Church

Two weeks ago.

A church in Palm Beach, Florida.

What was the sermon about?

I'd rather not get into it, frankly.

May 13, 2011, interview in Rolling Stone *magazine*
Discussing the last time he went to church

Leaks I

I will tell you that not within the meeting,

But outside of the meeting,

Somebody released it. It should have never been—

Number one, shouldn't have even entered paper.

But it should have never have been released.

But I read what was released

And I think it's a disgrace.

I think it's an absolute disgrace.

January 11, 2017, news conference
Answering a reporter's question about an intelligence briefing
concerning the so-called Trump dossier

Leaks II

I called, as you know, Mexico.

It was a very confidential, classified call,

But I called Mexico.

And in calling Mexico,

I figured, oh, well, that's nice.

Spoke to the president of Mexico.

I had a good call.

All of a sudden,

It's out for the world to see.

It's supposed to be secret.

It's supposed to be either confidential

Or classified, in that case.

Same thing with Australia.

All of a sudden, people are finding out

Exactly what took place.

February 16, 2017, news conference
Answering a reporter's question about Michael Flynn

Editor's Note: *It is the nature of words, especially in our electronic age, that what at the moment seems like "a good call" in private can be transformed in a different, public, context into an embarrassment. Trump captures this modern dilemma beautifully.*

And Ain't Nobody Got Time For That

I talked about anchor babies

At one news conference.

And one of the reporters,

Actually from ABC, said,

That's a derogatory term.

I said, why? He said, well, it's stronger.

He didn't know why.

And then I said, well,

What would you call them?

The babies of undocumented immigrants.

He gave me like a seven- or eight-word definition.

I said, we don't have time for that.

I'm sorry. We don't have time for that.

Now, look, I can be

The most politically correct person

That you have ever interviewed.

It takes too much time.

January 3, 2016, interview on CBS' Face the Nation
Discussing political correctness

Coke Or Pepsi

I like a little caffeine.

People assume I'm a boiler

Ready to explode,

But I actually have very low blood pressure,

Which is shocking to people.

I'll drink water.

Sometimes tomato juice, which I like.

Sometimes orange juice, which I like.

I'll drink different things.

But the Coke or Pepsi boosts you up a little.

May 13, 2011, interview in Rolling Stone *magazine*

Make A Deal

Then if we cannot make a deal—

Which I believe we will be able to,

And which I would prefer being able to—

But if we cannot make a deal—

I would like you to say,

I would prefer being able to—

Some people, the one thing they took out

Of your last story, you know, some people,

The fools and the haters, they said,

"Oh, Trump doesn't want to protect you."

I would prefer that we be able to continue,

But if we are not going to be reasonably reimbursed

For the tremendous cost of protecting these

Massive nations with tremendous wealth—

You have the tape going on?

July 20, 2016, recorded interview with the New York Times
*Discussing whether international allies should reimburse the U.S. for
the cost of American military protection*

For America

I'm very proud of

My company.

As you too know, I know

I built a very great company.

But if I become president,

I couldn't care less about

My company.

It's peanuts.

I want to use that same

Up here, whatever it may be

To make America rich again

And to make America great again.

I have Ivanka, and Eric and Don sitting there.

Run the company, kids, have a good time.

I'm going to do it for America.

II.

LOVE

I've known her—from an ample nation—
Choose One—
Then—close the Valves of her attention—
Like Stone—

—Emily Dickinson

At this point, it's to many people's
advantage to like me.

—Donald Trump

How Do I Back Thee?

I want to just let you know,

I am so behind you.

And I know maybe sometimes

You haven't gotten the backing that you've wanted,

And you're going to get so much backing.

Maybe you're going to say,

Please don't give us so much backing.

Mr. President,

Please,

We don't need that much backing.

But you're going to have that.

January 21, 2017, speech at CIA headquarters
Langley, Virginia

Editor's Note: *"Having someone's back" has become a cliché. Leave it to Trump to take that cliché, subvert it, hint at its dangers, and turn it into something marvelous and new: "Please don't give us so much backing."*

Super Bowl

I got a standing ovation.

In fact,

They said it was the biggest standing ovation

Since Peyton Manning

Had won the Super Bowl

And they said it was equal.

I got a standing ovation.

It lasted for a long period of time.

January 25, 2017, interview with David Muir
ABC News' World News Tonight
In reference to his speech at the CIA on January 21, 2017

My Hands Are Normal Hands

A hand with little fingers

Coming out of a stem

Like, *little.*

Look at my hands. They're fine.

Nobody other than Graydon Carter

Years ago used to use that.

My hands are normal hands.

During a debate, he was losing,

And he said, "Oh, he has small hands

And therefore, you know what that means."

This was not me. This was Rubio that said,

"He has small hands and you know

What that means." Okay? So, he started it.

So, what I said a couple of days later—

And what happened is

I was on line shaking hands with supporters,

And one of my supporters got up and he said,

"Mr. Trump, you have strong hands.

You have good-sized hands."

And then another one would say,

"You have great hands, Mr. Trump,

I had no idea." I said, "What do you mean?"

He said, "I thought you were like deformed,

And I thought you had small hands."

I had fifty people—is that a correct statement?

I mean people were writing, "How are Mr. Trump's

hands?"

My hands are fine. You know, my hands are normal.

Slightly large, actually. In fact,

I buy a slightly smaller than large glove, okay?

No, but I did this because everybody was saying to me,

"Oh, your hands are very nice.

They are normal."

March 21, 2016, interview with the Washington Post *editorial board*
Discussing a New Yorker *magazine cover illustration*

Editor's Note: *In a few short lines, Trump has managed a delightful little play on the last line of e. e. cummings' "somewhere i have never travelled" ("nobody, not even the rain, has such small hands").*

17 People

You know, when you have

So many people running—we had 17

And then they started to drop.

Ding.

 Bing.

I love it.

I love it.

And you'll be losing a lot

Over the next little while.

I would imagine.

December 8, 2015, remarks at USS Yorktown
Mount Pleasant, South Carolina
Discussing the other GOP presidential candidates

Ode To Abraham

Well, I think Lincoln succeeded for numerous reasons.

He was a man who was of great intelligence,

Which most presidents would be.

But he was a man of great intelligence,

But he was also a man that did something

That was a very vital thing to do at that time.

Ten years before or twenty years before,

What he was doing would never

Have even been thought possible.

So he did something that was a very

Important thing to do,

And especially at that time.

April 2, 2016, interview with the Washington Post

Hillary And Abe

She lied. Now she's blaming the lie

On the late, great Abraham Lincoln.

That's one that I haven't—

Ok, Honest Abe, Honest Abe never lied.

That's the good thing.

That's the big difference

Between Abraham Lincoln and you.

That's a big, big difference.

We're talking about some difference.

October 9, 2016, presidential debate
St. Louis, Missouri
Reacting to Hillary Clinton saying that her comment about public
opinions versus private opinions was inspired by the movie Lincoln

A Big Heart

They are here

Illegally.

They shouldn't be

Very worried.

I do have a

Big heart.

January 25, 2017, interview with David Muir
ABC News' World News Tonight
Discussing "dreamers," the children of illegal immigrants

A Lot Of Love

As far as people—Jewish people—

So many friends,

A daughter who happens to be here right now,

A son-in-law,

And three beautiful grandchildren.

I think that you're going to see

A lot different United States of America

Over the next three,

four,

or eight years.

I think

A lot of good things are happening,

And

You're going to see a lot of love.

You're going to see a lot of love.

February 15, 2017
Remarks in joint conference with Israeli PM Benjamin Netanyahu
The White House
Answering a question about anti-Semitism in the United States

You Might Be Persian

So it was a terrible deal.

It was a terrible negotiation.

It was negotiated by people

That are poor negotiators

Against great negotiators.

Persians being great negotiators, okay?

It's one of those things.

You might be Persian.

April 2, 2016, interview with the Washington Post
Discussing the Iran nuclear deal

A Love Story

But it is amazing,

Doing a story—a love story—

On how great we are together—

And by the way, we're stronger today

Than we ever were before,

Which is good, but it's a love story.

It's a love story on our one year.

And if I did that,

She would've added that—

It would've been the headline.

And who would've done that

If you're doing this

And you're one of the top shows

On television.

These people are horrible people.

They're horrible, horrible liars.

And interestingly,

It happens to appear

26 days

Before our very important election,

Isn't that amazing?

October 13, 2016, rally
West Palm Beach, Florida
Responding to a People Magazine *reporter's sexual*
harassment accusation

Poorly Educated

So we won the evangelicals.

We won with young.

We won with old.

We won with highly educated.

We won with poorly educated—

I love the poorly educated!

February 23, 2016, Nevada Primary victory speech
Washington, D.C.
Discussing the primary results

Editor's Note: *Few have taken Trump seriously as a Christian poet, but they should, and "Poorly Educated" is a good example of why, as the repeated "we won" of the first five lines becomes transformed, in Christian charity, to "I love the poorly educated!" in one of his most inspiring short poems.*

Women

She came out with that—

She came out—

Remember, she wrote—she said,

"He's got a—he's demonstrated

A penchant"—*I demonstrated*—

"A penchant for sexism."

Can you believe it?

Me?

Nobody respects women

More than Donald Trump.

That I can tell you.

May 8, 2016, interview on ABC's This Week
Omaha, Nebraska (Taped)
*Responding to George Stephanopoulos's question about prominent
Republicans refusing to endorse him*

High Society

I have Palm Beach,

I have Mar-a-Lago.

I deal with society.

Society loves me,

And I can act differently

For different people.

February 18, 2016, CNN Townhall
Columbia, South Carolina
Responding to Anderson Cooper's question about whether his tone
will be different if he becomes president

Mexico

I would then say—

Who's going to pay

For the wall? And people

Would all scream out—

Twenty-five, thirty thousand people,

Because no one's ever had crowds

Like Trump has had.

You know that.

You don't like to report that,

But that's okay.

Okay, now he agrees.

Finally, he agrees.

But, I say, who's going to pay for the wall?

And they will scream out—

Mexico.

January 11, 2017, press conference
New York, New York
Responding to a reporter's question on a border wall

Editor's Note: *The poem "Mexico" showcases two trademark Trump touches—the invitation to audience participation when the poem is read aloud—and the ending on a single word that all can exclaim: Mexico.*

Honesty

Now, the big story—

The retraction was, like, where?

Was it a line?

Or do they even bother putting it in?

So I only like to say that because

I love honesty.

I like honest reporting.

January 21, 2017, speech at CIA headquarters
Langley, Virginia
In reference to a Time Magazine *story that said Trump had removed a*
bust of Martin Luther King, Jr. from the Oval Office

I Cherish Women

I cherish women.

I want to help women.

I'm going to be able

To do things for women

That no other candidate

Would be able to do.

August 9, 2015, CNN interview
Responding to the backlash against his criticism of Megyn Kelly's
debate moderator performance

Editor's Note: *The word "cherish" bears the weight of this poem and is also key to its mystery—does Trump mean that he has affection for women? Or does "cherish" here follow Merriam Webster's second definition, "to entertain or harbor in the mind deeply and resolutely," as one cherishes a memory? A still more intriguing possibility lies in an outmoded third definition from Webster's American Dictionary of the English Language: "To treat in a manner to encourage growth, by protection, aid, attendance, or supplying nourishment; as, to cherish tender plants."*

The Problem With Republicans

The problem with the Republicans,

They have two sides.

The smaller side is very strong

And the other side is always agreeing.

October 18, 2015, interview on Fox News Sunday
New York, New York
Responding to Chris Wallace's question on the debt limit

III.

BEAUTY

And then my heart with pleasure fills,
And dances with the daffodils.

—William Wordsworth

Part of the beauty of me is that
I am very rich.

—Donald Trump

Morning Routine I

I get up, take a shower and wash my hair.

Then

I read the newspapers

Watch the news on television,

and slowly the hair dries.

It takes about an hour. I don't use a blow dryer.

Once it's dry I comb it.

Once I have it the way I like it—even though nobody

else likes it—I spray it.

I spray it and it's good for the day.

2004 Playboy Magazine *interview*

Morning Routine II

Ok, what I do is,

Wash it with Head and Shoulders.

I don't dry it, though.

I let it dry by itself.

It takes about an hour.

Then I read papers and things.

This morning I read in the *New York Post*

About Jerry Seinfeld

Backing out of his commitment

To do a benefit for my son Eric's charity.

I've never been a big fan of Jerry Seinfeld—

Never dug him, in the true sense—

But when I did *The Marriage Ref*,

Which was his show and a total disaster,

I did him a big favor.

Then he did this.

It's a disgrace.

May 13, 2011, interview in Rolling Stone *magazine*

Editor's Note: *"Never dug him, in the true sense," is a classic Trump line that layers meaning upon meaning.*

Barack Obama

Wrote me,

By the way,

A very beautiful letter

In the drawer of the desk.

Very beautiful.

And I appreciate it.

January 25, 2017
Interview with David Muir, ABC News' World News Tonight

All The Dress Shops Are Sold Out In Washington

We are going to have an unbelievable,

Perhaps record-setting turnout

For the inauguration,

And there will be plenty of

Movie and entertainment stars.

All the dress shops are sold out in Washington.

It's hard to find a great dress

For this inauguration.

Quoted in a January 9, 2017 New York Times *article*

Editor's Note: *Note the masterful use of a negative image—empty dress shops—to create a positive image—inaugural balls packed with gilded women in "great" dresses.*

Hairspray

He's got a problem with the carbon footprint.

You can't use hairspray.

Because hairspray is going to affect the ozone.

I'm trying to figure this out,

Let's see, I'm in my room

In New York City

And I want to put a little spray

So I can—right?

But I hear that they don't want me to use hairspray

They want me to use the pump

Because the other one—

Which I really like better than going

Bing, Bing, Bing,

And then it comes out in big blobs, right,

And it's stuck in your hair and you say

Oh my God, I've got to take a shower again

My hair is all screwed up. Right?—

I want to use hairspray.

They say, "Don't use hairspray.

It's bad for the ozone."

So I'm sitting in this concealed apartment,

This concealed unit—

You know, I really do live in a very nice apartment, right?

But it's sealed!

It's beautiful!

And I don't think anything gets out—

And I'm not supposed to be using hairspray.

December 30, 2015, campaign speech
Hilton Head, South Carolina
Discussing President Obama's position on global warming and
humans' carbon footprint

Editor's Note: *The interconnectedness of everything—or not—is Trump's theme here, where even hairspray has become politicized. He asks us to consider whether what the poet does in his "concealed unit," his "very nice apartment," which is "sealed," still has an alleged effect on the ozone or whether environmental hectoring is doing away with our privacy and intimate consumer choices.*

It's My Hair I

I don't wear a toupee,

It's my hair,

I swear.

August 25, 2016
Greenville, South Carolina
Campaign rally

It's My Hair II

I will never

Change this hairstyle,

I like it.

It fits my head.

Those who criticize me

Are only losers and envy people.

And it is not a wig,

It's my hair.

Do you want to touch it?

February 2014 interview with Brazilian magazine Veja

Space

This is infinity—

It could be infinity—

We don't really—don't know—

But it could be—

There's gotta be something—

But it could be infinity—

Right?

June 30, 2017, remarks at the signing of an Executive Order on the
National Space Council
The White House

Editor's Note: *In seven deceptively simple lines, Trump expresses a cosmological vision of humility and hope that deftly refutes the existentialist despair, especially the sort we associate with Jean-Paul Sartre.*

The Beauty Sake

I look at things

For the art sake

And the beauty sake

And

For the deal sake.

July 11, 1988, interview with New York Magazine
Discussing his acquisition of "toys" or "works of art"

The Canvas And The Coal Mine

I do what I do out of pure enjoyment.

Hopefully, nobody does it better.

There's a beauty to making a great deal.

It's my canvas. And I like painting it.

I like the challenge and tell the story

Of the coal miner's son.

The coal miner gets black-lung disease,

His son gets it, then *his* son.

If *I* had been the son of a coal miner,

I would have left the damn mines.

But most people don't have the imagination—or

whatever—

To leave their mine.

They don't have "it."

March 14, 1990, Playboy Magazine *interview*

Editor's Note: *If there is an unmistakably classic Trump poem it is "The Canvas and the Coal Mine," which moves with sinuous grace from the "beauty of making a great deal," to the defiant raging, a la Dylan Thomas, against the black lung tyranny of "the damn mines."*

Into The Air

Pressure doesn't

Upset my sleep.

I like throwing balls

Into the air—

And I dream

Like a baby.

March 14, 1990, interview in Playboy Magazine
Discussing his sleeping habits

Can You Imagine

Can you imagine

How controversial I'd be?

You think about him

And the women.

How about me

With the women?

Can you imagine?

1999 CNBC interview
Addressing rumors of his presidential aspirations and comparing
himself to President Bill Clinton

The Day Lawrence Cried

Remember this crazy man, Lawrence O'Donnell—

He's a total crazy nut—

He said, Donald Trump only made a million dollars

With *The Apprentice*. I said, A million dollars?

You know, when you have a show

That's essentially number one

Almost every time it goes on,

You can name it—

So anyway, when they added it all up—

And these are certified numbers,

Because you have to do certified numbers—

It came out to $213 million. Okay?

That's what I made on *The Apprentice*.

That's just—and that's one of my small things.

That's what I made. You know?

So it was put at $213 million, and it was certified.

And your friend Joe in the morning said,

There's no way he only made. . .

They had a big fight, and O'Donnell,

Lawrence O'Donnell started crying.

I never saw anything like it.

Do you remember? He started crying.

He actually started crying.

April 2, 2016, interview with the Washington Post
Discussing MSNBC TV host Lawrence O'Donnell

Ernest Hemingway

Somebody said

I'm the Ernest Hemingway

Of 140 characters.

November 20, 2015, forum at Wofford College in Spartanburg, South Carolina
Discussing his use of Twitter

Editor's Note: *This wry homage to the master, "Papa" Hemingway—underlines how Hemingway the novelist was in so many ways the model for Trump the poet.*

A Beautiful Thing

And you'll have health plans,

You'll have healthcare plans,

That you've never even—

I know a lot about healthcare,

You know a lot about healthcare,

They'll come up with plans that

You've never even heard about

That will be so good.

They'll have a lot of competition,

They'll have a lot of new ideas

That people don't even think about today.

And it'll be a beautiful thing.

April 23, 2017, Associated Press interview

Editor's Note: *Trump's poetry is often centered on the search for beauty and offers many parallels to Keats—never more so than in the famous line "Beauty is truth, truth beauty," which could easily be mistaken for a line of Trump's.*

Truly Great

We have a chance

To be truly great,

Truly great,

Truly great—

I don't mean a little bit,

I mean truly great

Again.

August 25, 2016
Greenville, South Carolina
Campaign Rally

Editor's Note: *Trump, like Picasso, is an artist who often brings "primitive" influences to modernism. Here he evokes the rhythm of the tom-tom (Truly great, Truly great) in an extraordinary seven-line verse.*

Snowflake Reporter

She didn't almost fall to the ground.

He got in her way. And by the way,

She was grabbing me!

Am I supposed to press charges against her?

Oh, my arm is hurting.

Anderson, my arm is just killing me.

It's never been the same.

March 29, 2016, CNN Townhall
Milwaukee, Wisconsin
Responding to Anderson Cooper's question about reporter Michelle
Fields' assault accusation against campaign manager Corey
Lewandowski, who grabbed her by the arm

Editor's Note: *Trump, like Kipling, is a "masculine" poet. In "Snowflake Reporter" he takes aim at the new generation of reporters whom he considers much softer than the hardboiled newsmen of his youth.*

Plaza Story

If they put me on the cover

Of the *Daily News*,

They sell more papers!

They put me on the cover

Of the *Daily News* today

With wars breaking out!

You know why?

Malcolm Forbes got

Thrown out of the Plaza by me!

You know the story about me

And Malcolm Forbes,

When I kicked him out of the Plaza hotel?

No?

Well,

I did.

September 1990 interview in Vanity Fair
Discussing a New York Daily News *article about* Forbes *dropping him
off its richest men list*

Good Wall

It would be tall, it would be powerful,

We would make it very good looking.

It would be as good as a wall's got to be,

And people will not be climbing over that wall,

Believe me.

September 3, 2015, interview on The Hugh Hewitt Show
Discussing a border wall

Editor's Note: *An exquisite rejoinder to Robert Frost's "Mending Wall"*
("Something there is that doesn't love a wall") which makes a pat,
clean case that good fences do indeed make good neighbors.

Big Crowds

I've seen crowds before.

Big,

Big crowds.

That was some crowd.

When I looked at the numbers

That happened to come in from all of the various

sources,

We had the biggest audience

In the history of inaugural speeches.

I said the men and women

That I was talking to

Who came out and voted

Will never be forgotten again.

Therefore I won't allow you

Or other people like you

To demean that crowd and

To demean the people that came to Washington, DC,

From faraway places

Because they like me.

But more importantly

They like what I'm saying.

January 25, 2017, interview with David Muir
ABC News' World News Tonight
In reference to Inauguration Day attendance

Loretta & Bill I

In the back of her airplane, while on the runway

—Remember he was there

—He was going to play golf.

Oh, oh gee, there's the Attorney General. Let me go

say hello

—Plane's on the runway. Let me go say hello to the

Attorney General.

He never got to play golf, I understand.

And it was Arizona, a place I love,

But the weather was about a hundred and some odd

degrees

—He's not gonna play. He was never there to play

golf, folks, don't be foolish.

October 13, 2016, speech
West Palm Beach, Florida
Discussing President Bill Clinton's meeting with Attorney General
Loretta Lynch on a tarmac

Loretta & Bill II

They met for 39 minutes.

Remember he said, we talked golf

And we talked about our grandchildren.

Three minutes for the grandchildren,

Two minutes for the golf,

Then they sat there and they twiddled their thumbs.

October 13, 2016, speech
West Palm Beach, Florida
Discussing President Bill Clinton's meeting with Attorney General
Loretta Lynch on a tarmac

Editor's Note: *The paired Loretta and Bill poems are an indirect tribute to golf, a game Trump loves, knows well, plays well, and, as these poems reveal, can write about with wonderful insight.*

You're Fired

There's a beauty

In those

Two words.

When you utter

Those words,

There's very little

That can be said.

There's a succinctness

To those words.

March 28, 2004, interview with the San Francisco Chronicle
Discussing his catchphrase, "You're fired."

I Like Bullets

I like bullets

Or

I like as little

As possible.

I don't need,

You know,

200-page reports

On something that

Can be handled

On a page.

That

I can tell you.

January 18, 2017, interview with Axios
New York, New York
Discussing briefings

IV.

DEATH

With morning wakes the will, and cries,
"Thou shalt not be the fool of loss."

—Lord Alfred Tennyson

I'm a survivor—a survivor of success,
which is a very rare thing indeed.

—Donald Trump

The Grudge

I like to do the right thing and help people.

But when people are disloyal to me—

I have a couple of instances of well-known people,

Where I'd help them out,

But when I needed a favor,

Not a big favor in this one case,

This guy didn't want to do it.

That's fifteen years ago.

I haven't spoken to him since.

He died.

He's dead mentally.

In other words, for me, they don't exist.

I hold a grudge.

I have the longest memory.

I always kick back.

I believe in that.

Electric Chair

What would happen to me if I did that?

Electric chair, I think.

The electric chair.

If I did that, can you imagine?

October 31, 2016, rally
Flint, Michigan
Commenting on Donna Brazile debate question leak to Clinton

The Pope

The Pope

I hope

Can only be scared

By God.

August 19, 2015, interview with CNN

Editor's Note: *We touched before on Trump as a Christian poet. In "The Pope" he makes a tentative, but memorable, assertion about the Catholic faith in four pithy lines that would have been the envy of Gerard Manley Hopkins.*

Scalia

We lost a great one in Scalia,

Justice Scalia,

And that was a great surprise.

But this president,

This next president,

Could have as many as five.

Hard to believe.

I don't believe

There's ever been as many as five!

June 21, 2016, meeting with Evangelical leaders
New York, New York

Editor's Note: *For a poet, repetition is a tool, but also a risk, which Trump takes often to delightful effect, as in "Scalia" with the phrase "as many as five."*

Critics

I don't call them critics.

I call them fools.

January 25, 2017, interview with David Muir
ABC News' World News Tonight
In reference to critics' reaction to taking oil from Iran

Editor's Note: *Trump, like many poets, respects doers, not critics. In this two-line masterpiece, he makes his feelings plain.*

The World Is An Angry Place

The world is a mess.

The world is as angry as it gets.

What?

You think this is gonna cause a little more anger?

The world is an angry place.

January 25, 2017, interview with David Muir
ABC News' World News Tonight
In reference to the ban on refugees coming into the U.S.

Editor's Note: *As an exercise in Christian realism, "The World Is an Angry Place" is something of a masterpiece. It also carries echoes of the bleak, sardonic verse of Stephen Crane, whose influence on Trump has been too little noted.*

Nuclear War

It's like thinking the Titanic can't sink.

Too many countries have nuclear weapons;

Nobody knows where they're all pointed,

What button it takes to launch them.

The bomb Harry Truman dropped on Hiroshima

Was a toy next to today's. We have thousands of weapons

Pointed at us and nobody even knows

If they're going to go in the right direction.

They've never really been tested.

These jerks in charge don't know how to paint a wall,

And we're relying on them to shoot nuclear missiles

to Moscow.

What happens if they don't go there?

March 14, 1990, Playboy *interview*
Discussing the possibility of nuclear war

Editor's Note: *Even as early as 1990, the image of the "wall" (which here the "jerks in charge don't know how to paint") loomed large in Trump's imagination.*

The Power Of What's Going To Happen

Nuclear is powerful;

My uncle explained that to me

Many, many years ago,

The power

And that was thirty-five years ago;

He would explain

The power of what's going to happen

And he was right—

Who would have thought?

July 21, 2015, campaign rally
Sun City, South Carolina

Those People Have To Be Worried

We have really bad people that are here.

Those people have to be worried

'Cause they're getting out.

We're gonna get them out.

We're gonna get 'em out

Fast.

January 25, 2017, interview with David Muir
ABC News' World News Tonight
Discussing "dreamers," the children of illegal immigrants

To See Bill Gates

We're losing a lot of people

Because of the Internet.

We have to go see Bill Gates

And a lot of different people

That really understand what's happening.

We have to talk to them about,

Maybe in certain areas,

Closing that Internet up in some way.

Somebody will say,

"Oh freedom of speech, freedom of speech."

These are foolish people.

We have a lot of foolish people.

December 7, 2015, campaign rally
Mount Pleasant, South Carolina
Discussing ISIS recruitment

It

We need that thinking.

We have the opposite thinking.

We have losers.

We have losers.

We have people that don't have

It.

June 16, 2015, campaign announcement
New York, New York
After disclosing his net worth

The Mantle Of Anger

First of all, Nikki this afternoon said

I'm a friend of hers. Actually a close friend.

And wherever you are sitting Nikki,

I'm a friend. We're friends. That's good.

But she did say there was anger.

And I could say, oh, I'm not angry.

I'm very angry because our country is being run horribly

And I will gladly accept the mantle of anger.

January 14, 2016, Republican presidential debate
North Charleston, South Carolina
Responding to a question about South Carolina Governor Nikki Haley's
comment that Republicans should resist "the siren call of anger"

The Birds

We bought a whole series of birds

For the suites in the Plaza Hotel.

These are real, live birds—all sorts of little birds

Flying around in the suites. Some people walk in,

They don't believe what they're seeing.

Usually they're just little artificial birds.

These are real birds. And we have to be very careful,

David, with who we let go into the suites.

Sometimes a high roller wants to come to New York,

And they want to go into the Plaza Hotel,

And I'll never let a high roller from Atlantic City

Go into the suite in The Plaza

Where we have these live birds

Because the birds won't be alive very long.

November 10, 1988, interview with David Letterman

Loser

They can always

Do that

And then they'll—

Then they'll just

Lose everything and

That would be the—

That would be the work

Of a loser.

March 2, 2016, Super Tuesday victory speech
New York, New York
Responding to reporter's question about whether conservatives will
vote for third-party candidate

Nasty

I can only tell you

What I would like to do.

I would love to be able to

Get along with everybody.

Right now, the world is a mess.

But I think by the time we finish,

I think it's going to be

A lot better place to live.

And I can tell you that,

Speaking for myself,

By the time I'm finished,

It's going to be a lot better place to live in—

Because right now

It's *nasty*.

April 12, 2017, press conference
Answering a reporter's question about Russian president Vladimir Putin

Editor's Note: *During the 2016 presidential campaign, Hillary Clinton took the word "nasty" and boasted about being a "nasty woman" as though this were a positive trait, somewhat similar to the way gangster rappers use the word "bad" to mean "good." Trump, both politically and poetically, is more conservative and uses words like "nasty" with precision and respect for their literal meaning.*

A Level Of Evil

But we're going to do great things.

We're going to do great things.

We've been fighting these wars for longer

Than any wars we've ever fought.

We have not used the real abilities that we have.

We've been restrained.

We have to get rid of ISIS.

Have to get rid of ISIS.

We have no choice.

Radical Islamic terrorism.

And I said it yesterday—

It has to be eradicated just off the face of the Earth.

This is evil.

This is evil.

And you know, I can understand the other side.

We can all understand the other side.

There can be wars between countries,

There can be wars.

You can understand what happened.

This is something nobody can even understand.

This is a level of evil that we haven't seen.

And you're going to go to it, and

You're going to do a phenomenal job.

But we're going to end it.

It's time.

It's time right now to end it.

January 21, 2017, speech at CIA headquarters
Langley, Virginia
First official visit to a government agency as president

Editor's Note: *Walt Whitman is yet another influence on Trump, especially as a war poet. Trump's repetition of ISIS, "this is evil," and "there can be wars," will likely put many readers in mind of Whitman's similar repetition of "Beat! beat! drums!—blow! bugles! blow!"*

"Keep the Oil"

The old expression,

"To the victor belong the spoils"—

You remember.

I always used to say,

Keep the oil.

I wasn't a fan of Iraq.

I didn't want to go into Iraq.

But I will tell you,

When we were in,

We got out wrong.

And I always said,

In addition to that,

Keep the oil.

Now, I said it for economic reasons.

But if you think about it,

If we kept the oil

You probably wouldn't have ISIS

Because that's where they made their

Money in the first place.

So we should have kept the oil.

But okay.

Maybe you'll have another chance.

But the fact is,

Should have kept the oil.

January 21, 2017, speech at CIA headquarters
Langley, Virginia
First official visit to the agency as president

Chicago

They're gonna have to get tougher

And stronger

And smarter.

But they gotta fix the problem.

I don't want to have thousands of people

Shot in a city

Where essentially

I'm the president.

I love Chicago.

I know Chicago.

And Chicago is a great city,

Can be a great city.

January 25, 2017, interview with David Muir
ABC News' World News Tonight
Discussing crime in Chicago

Editor's Note: *Poets are competitive, measuring themselves against other poets. In "Chicago" Trump makes his case to displace Carl Sandburg as the city's poet laureate: "I love Chicago / I know Chicago. / And Chicago is a great city, / Can be a great city," if it has the right poet, he implies; one who also happens to be president.*

China

Our country is in serious trouble.

We don't have victories anymore.

We used to have victories,

But we don't have them.

When was the last time

Anybody saw us beating, let's say,

China in a trade deal?

They kill us.

I beat China all the time.

June 16, 2015, presidential bid announcement
New York, New York

Libel

They should at least try

To get it right.

And if they don't do a retraction,

They should,

They should, you know, have a form

Of a trial.

I don't want to impede free press,

By the way.

The last thing I would want to do

Is that.

But I mean I can only speak for—

I probably get more—

Do I, I mean, you would know,

Do I get more publicity

Than any human being on the earth?

Okay?

I mean, she kills me, this one—

That's okay, nice woman.

March 21, 2016, interview with the Washington Post *editorial board*
Discussing his position on libel; pointing out Ruth Marcus

Problems I

Many, many problems.

When I was campaigning, I said

It's not a good situation.

Now that I see it—

Including with our

Intelligence briefings—

We have problems

That a lot of people

Have no idea how bad they are,

How serious they are,

Not only

Internationally,

But when you come right here.

February 17, 2017
Answering a reporter's question about national security

Problems II

Right now there is a fear, and there are problems—

There are certainly problems.

But ultimately, I hope that there won't be a fear

And there won't be problems,

And the world can get along.

That would be the ideal situation.

It's crazy what's going on—whether it's the Middle East

Or you look at—no matter where the—Ukraine—

You look at—whatever you look at,

It's got problems, so many problems.

And ultimately,

I believe that we

Are going to get rid

Of most of those problems,

And there won't be fear of anybody.

That's the way it should be.

April 12, 2017, press conference
Answering a reporter's question about whether NATO
should play a role in Syria

Problems III

So look,

Look,

Our country has a lot of problems.

Believe me.

I know what the problems are

Even better than you do.

They're deep problems,

They're serious problems.

We don't need more.

January 25, 2017, interview with David Muir
ABC News' World News Tonight

Editor's Note: *Trump's famous "Problems" triptych is a brilliant demonstration of poetic structure in three parts. It begins with the world having "many, many problems." It moves to getting "rid of most of those problems....That's the way it should be." And concludes with the breathtakingly plangent: "We don't need more."*

Contract

But I'm really good at looking at a

Contract

And finding things within a

Contract

That even if they're bad, I would police that

Contract

So tough that they don't have a chance. As bad as the

Contract

Is, I will be so tough on that

Contract.

August 16, 2015, interview on NBC's Meet the Press
Discussing the Iran nuclear deal

Fight

They didn't want to knock out

The oil

Because of what it's going to do

To the carbon footprint.

We don't fight like we used

To fight.

We used to fight

To win.

Now we fight for no reason

Whatsoever.

We don't even know

What we're doing.

March 10, 2016, Republican debate in Miami, Florida
Responding to a question from Hugh Hewitt on ISIS

Fight Fire With Fire

When they're shooting—

When they're chopping off the heads of our people

And other people,

When they're chopping off the heads of people

Because they happen to be

A Christian in the Middle East,

When ISIS is doing things

That nobody has ever heard of

Since Medieval times,

Would I feel strongly about waterboarding?

As far as I'm concerned we have to

Fight fire with fire.

January 25, 2017, interview with David Muir
ABC News' World News Tonight

Editor's Note: *Trump's poetic essence—the quality that makes him inimitable—is captured dramatically in the arresting rhythm and imagery of these three lines—When they're chopping off the heads of our people And other people, When they're chopping off the heads of people — lines that strike not only at the heart of the matter, but at its head.*

A Promise To Bore

Yes,

Always to fight.

My natural inclination

Is to win.

And after I win,

I will be so

Presidential

That you won't even recognize me.

You'll be falling asleep,

You'll be so

Bored.

April 2, 2016, interview with the Washington Post
Answering a question about whether his instinct is to be combative

Editor's Note: *One thing is for certain. Trump as a poet can never bore. He is the nation's unofficial poet laureate.*

AFTERWORD

H. W. Crocker III

When I read English at UC San Diego, my favorite poet was Rudyard Kipling.

But if you were to ask me who my favorite living poet is, I would say, without equivocation, Donald J. Trump.

From the pith of "Sad!" or "You're Fired" to the studied ambiguity of "Bigly" or "Big League," Donald Trump is a master wordsmith—and, like the greatest poets, a truly memorable one. "Lone Ranger" and "Electric Chair" are poems that, once read, are impossible to forget.

Trump's free verse is subversive on many levels, but also affirms certain traditionalist conventions. In this, he is very much like Hemingway, Trump's counterpoint in prose. Both use deceptively simple, impressionistic language and repetition to stylistically revolutionary, but structurally conservative, effect.

What interests me even more in Trump is how transgressive he is; how he has bulldozed regnant powers and clichés.

We have heard quite a lot about how Trump represents the sudden eruption of a suppressed nationalist populism against the established liberal consensus—a consensus that enveloped both Democrats and Republicans who essentially agreed on immigration, trade, internationalism, and big government, differing perhaps on details but not the big picture.

But we have not heard nearly enough about how Trump's poetry has overturned the corrupt academic-leftist monopoly on literature that has enshrined the unintelligible; the narrowly, stupidly feminist, Marxist, racist-identity-politics Left; and the government-subsidized rubbish that we might otherwise be spared—all of it written in a strangely bureaucratic newspeak celebrating a perpetual adolescent rebellion against a white male Christian American establishment that (a) only ever really existed in the Left's overheated imagination and (b) as far as it did exist has been in rapid retreat, if not entirely routed, over the last half century.

Trump knows this. He is far more in tune with the culture than most contemporary poets; his historical scope of reference is much vaster: like Matthew Arnold he recognizes the "melancholy, long, withdrawing roar" of the sea of faith. With Cyril Connolly, he knows that "it is closing time in the gardens of the West." And like

Dylan Thomas, he believes in not going "gentle into that good night." He believes in raging "against the dying of the light."

But it is remarkable how temperate and measured his raging is. You will not find in the canon of Trump splenetic anger or foul-mouthed tirades. Anyone who has read Trump's poetry is struck by its economy of words; its precision; its respect for tradition; its focus on love, on greatness that elevates others. He is certainly, in this sense, the model conservative poet, and both far more of his time, and far more willing to take artistic risks, than T. S. Eliot.

Mentioning Eliot inevitably raises the question, as do several of the editor's notes, of Trump as a specifically Christian poet. I do not want to belabor this point, but it is an element of Trump's oeuvre that should not be ignored. Any poet, like Eliot or Trump, who seeks to restore the fonts of Western Civilization, must of necessity repair to Christian imagery and themes, the Christian vision. And in this too Trump is immensely subversive of the subsidized leftist-luvvie arts orthodoxy, which is far more suffocatingly conformist than the medieval Church ever was.

I am grateful to Rob Long for having compiled this wonderful and long-needed book. It will be my bedside companion for years to come.

About the Author

Rob Long, writer and co-executive producer of the much-beloved, long-running TV series *Cheers* and more recently of *Kevin Can Wait*, is the author of *Conversations with My Agent* and *Set Up, Joke, Set Up, Joke*. He is also a contributing editor to *National Review*, hosts the syndicated radio show *Martini Shot*, is a founder of the website Ricochet.com, and contributes to many publications, including the *Wall Street Journal* and the *Los Angeles Times*. A two-time Emmy Award and Golden Globe Award nominee, he divides his time between New York and Hollywood.